THE ART OF LOVE

Love Poems and Paintings
by Melinda Camber Porter

Writers and Readers Publishing, Incorporated
P.O. Box 461, Village Station
New York, NY 10014

c/o Airlift Book Company
26/28 Eden Grove
London N7 8EF
England

ISBN # 0-86316-167-7 Paperback
ISBN # 0-86316-168-5 Hardcover

1 2 3 4 5 6 7 8 9 0

Printed and bound in Singapore

"And we are put on earth a little space,
That we may learn to bear the beams of love"

William Blake
from *Songs of Innocence and Experience*

About

Melinda Camber Porter

A graduate of Oxford University with First Class Honors in Modern Languages, British writer Melinda Camber Porter is a woman of remarkable versatility.

As a journalist, she reported on cultural affairs for *The Times* in Paris. Contemporary French culture is the subject of her book *Through Parisian Eyes*, a series of interviews with some of the most compelling French artists and thinkers of our time. The *Boston Globe* describes it as "a particularly readable and brilliantly and uniquely compiled collection" while Joyce Carol Oates writes, "it is intriguing and very well done." A new paperback edition of the book will be released in October 1993 from Da Capo Press, Inc.

As a novelist and poet, Melinda Camber Porter has written many works including her recently completed book *Badlands*. Esteemed as "an extraordinary novel," by Louis Malle, *Badlands* is set on the Pine Ridge Reservation in South Dakota and has been described by Peter Matthiessen as "lyrical and unflinching on Native American issues."

A playwright and lyricist, she created the musical *Night Angel* and the comedy *Boat Child*. Her poetry and journalism have appeared in a variety of publications internationally. These publications include *The New Statesman*, *The Observer*, *The Times Literary Supplement*, *Le Monde* and *The Partisan Review*.

A life long painter, Melinda Camber Porter worked briefly at the National Portrait Gallery in London. Today, she continues to write for *The Times* from New York where she lives with her husband, Joe Flicek and their son, Robert.

for my darling husband, Joe Flicek,
and our darling son, Robert,
with love

Acknowledgements

I am deeply grateful to my publisher, Glenn Thompson, for being who he is: a man who takes risks, loves literature, acts with integrity and an outrageous sense of humour. He is one of the last true publishers left and is committed to making a real contribution to our culture. Also, my thanks go to Joellyn Ausanka for typing the manuscript with such meticulous care and to Terrie Dunkelberger for designing the book and cover. And my very special thanks goes to Deborah Dyson of *Writers and Readers*.

I'm perpetually grateful to my husband, Joe, who encourages and inspires me, daily.

First Love

He took me under

                the branches where the day lay black

    lay curved on the ground the branches

lazy back,

        under he took my hand over

my eyes and my lips

          war on his back

                on mine

into the night without word

            he opened

into my soul and touched

            lay breathless as birth

he took me into the night but the day

                coloured with purple;

I could not hold its liquid from out my eyes

                  his hand touched

the earth with blood and ice

            the flowers are purple sap.

He took me into the night under the trees we stayed

                    back to back

by the branches. I did not mind the blood

                pouring from the trees.

Seed Time

This white
seed blurted out its secret green
and the insects came thinking it was
already flowered.
It lay subtle as a broken vase
telling of shocked lines
natural curves
of the stone fed ripple.
Once egg shell smooth,
the new worm paths
are beauteous wrinkles
eroded rocks stuffed with years
of wind's breath.
The once white shell
opened and did not crumble.
It lay sculptured
on the earth clods
where I picked it up.
Now it lies in my glass.

Passion

life's details

        were whittled away

till only your face remained

      your body at night

        your words of extreme beauty

life woke up in the morning

        scrambled to lie with us

you walk away

        life walks out of my sight.

The Ordeal

the ordeal was erected inside the mind;
so there was no escape,
each limb cut off from the body's direction
moved out of tune;
the whirring of flesh and bone
was the only sound, and the ear
cut off from the mouth
could not make sense of it;
but it was not that; there was no outward sign,
only a tendency to burst into tears, day-long,
to see nothing, as the inner eye
had been cut from the eye,
to hope for someone
who had at one time directed the pain
onto one limb
so the pain of the other limbs had seemed slight.
but it was not that; for the ordeal was erected inside the mind.

In the Stillness

In the stillness
        pause between kissing
        pause when the sentence ends
and there is no new one to begin
in the gap when I have stopped, in the open wound
as we gaze at each other
at that moment I would hope we could look
each other quite
still, look at each other in the eye
the eye
and you would find peace
and I would find peace
        in the pause the still moments
would give you peace

Ritual Song

This is a time of wandering
Over the charred fields of time
The child time of wordless
Murmurings and even now though we talk

There is no one to listen,
No permanent friend to return to and leave
and return to.
And there is no city for
The skyscrapers smell of air;
There are no nooks except in the gutter.

There is the time of the desert
Drifting when the water of love
And soft buds and good touch
Grow in the death of the sun parched eye
As mirage
Forced into day by the black
Blown tongue.

This time of wandering
has climbed into song.

My Father's Shadow

When I awoke
my father's shadow had left my side
light was still of dreams
blue with labyrinthine passages of unplunged time.
I was lovely alone
holding in hand the flesh of rib.
When I awoke my father's shadow
had left my side.
I walked the streets
too open to sky
and in the narrow backstreets smudged with
man's passage felt cold fear of criminal
bending on the blue stone sea
reflecting opaque sky.
When I returned
my father's shadow hung in the cupboard.
The room emptied of light
was too cold to love in.
              I cried
                   for long hours.
Perhaps a moment before dawn
I came to sad dreams
             mangled by fear of falling
                  falling
onto flesh splitting stone shattering
rock below.

Calf

in the electric green
fields a calf is wrenched
from its redwhite mother
and taken to
a white cubicle
electric light
and pitch blackness
not the thick blue mottled-starred
night-sky to dream liquid
thoughts onto

this is no allegory

there is a lunge in her throat
and a lunge round her neck
the cubicle whites
of her eyes and bulb
shimmer in one kind of intensity

no allegory

the shriek of pain
silver too
sticks its pin into her slimmer tendons
outside the hunter
waits waiting
like her mother who hangs upside down
in her dreams
swirling in her cow eyes
with sight of her own death

but the fields at day are full
of others
and the electric green
tones into other yellows and reds
sometimes it is muzzy with pink
this is no allegory
touch the sky yourself
and feel how it hangs heavy
feel too the stickiness
of the green fields
your own death

Breaking Up

The moon is a circle, a scent of fear
in the black sky,
a tunnel of endless length.
Her stockings dangle empty on the sea swell
over the fishes' shimmering sides.

The moon is the white lie.
We weep for her when she wanes
Thinner than sharp blade,
And the pain is worse for us,
Deeper,
For the moon only hides and sways
In her steady sphere
While she sips the black clouds of our dust.

And last year we walked on her face
her pock marked
mask haunts our dreams,
broke up our dreams of her love.

No End in Sight

The cathedral windows, gothically curved
glide upwards; upwards I walk as the
paintings of glass light up, mad
mothers and similar child
  prophets,
    equinox blasted,
      spring blossomed,
        frost crushed,
          in one single moment.

To the organ suspended by streamers
I glide. There are no steps;
the marinous sea sips
sand
under my widening eyes.
There is no entry or exit,
  no end or beginning.
    This gothic glimmer
      flashes through centuries,
        got lodged in my heart
          where it stops the blood,
            passions the blood to flow.
              I resound in and around.

Sex Without Words

A letter to no one
was traced with the body.

Your mother and father
as you have never known them
some god deposed by centuries laughter

was addressed
and actually the Golden Age
landed in each port and doorway.

It needed a ritual
undressing again for the new
year and wiping ecstasy
sweat dry.

The gestures were done
with no one or politely

calculated the precise
moment to last no longer
than the seconds you mourn.

The Bridge of War

The pont du carrousel weeps
its own roots only a child would
not know the history of tears
that foam and ripple is
not a wound, that disappearance
of boats is no loss.

Yes, under the waves my
lost air your breath has already
misted other mirrors shaped
like women it was no loss
it is smiling and never mind
and what is a voice over which
no passengers can walk no
lovers cut short no friends
know the spoilt bliss.

When water speaks more kind
than mother or child it is no loss
when lovers leave it is growing
up there is no history of
tears no memory no self.

The Lover Abounds

My love,
I do repeat the abstract form
you take, for sometimes in the trees,
or in a face I feel to find you,
or in a written word, my love,
or when I saw
first eyes
and did not speak in questions.
Then, my love, you shift; I dare not
say you leave, for,
my loved one,
you die with my death.

And as you shift, finding
new stone, a picture or a face to
slide in, there I watch,
not touching you.

Or were you never there?
The tone behind all sight?
but never there?
and did you leave instead
a land bereft of love
where I should learn through
absence of your hold?

Last night
when the white moon
came close to earth
I saw your hands;
I knew that you had put her there.
But love, you did not talk to me,
Huddling in my own so weak
embrace all I could feel were bones.

And dare I take another?

My love, you are covering the sky
you are shaping forms in the clouds.
Must I step down from this
and never see your face?

A constellation of dead stars.
We had the dreams knocked from the skull,
and saw stars, so sick.

Birth

I   At first birth
    I rose from the sea
    through its blue underground combs
    I climbed
            till earth came covering me
    now
    curled in its earthy warmth
    new sea. Still silently still the sea
    like snow covering bulbs till spring rushes
    their veins.
    I too have no say
    nor can I speak of it.

II But of the sky I heard birds
    drank glimpses of new climb of blue
    Woke scared at night
    which seemed colour of day
    colour of earth.

III   My roots grew.

Growing the earth still held me still.

Wind moved me

but I could only grow high

A part of the earth

earth bound still

I can only grow nearer and nearer the sky

                                      alone unmoved

I can only grow

lonely

       and high.

IV   Sky melted to night

                      piling itself with light and dark

Grass rushed into green and gold and the

Same curly fence held back the cows that

Grazed near my field of earth

Worms birds rushed me through and away

Into their other fields flew homeless.

V   One night when the earth was black

I dreamt of my move

my roots withered

My eyes I covered in white

White tissue web of

animal fur and seeds of

dead fruits.

VI   The field in sway.

             Am I drunk on the thick

Green air of spring and night?

Stalk holds itself tight

              takes new swill of life

now sounds buzz in my veins

                red bleeds in my veins

now white enters my bark.

On the seventh day of this flooding change

I wrench out of the earth.

My dreams

crack my eyes

colours of

All I know caught in my eyes.

VII   When the field stays I will go

rise into a moving meet

into new walks

          of time.

The Cold of Stone

The pebbles commiserate
we are empty in silence.
They cannot move, can I?

I tried this dialogue
                    with the world
the only world
the only words I know.
The words sounded as silence
on the only silent world
of ice cocoon.

The pebbles commiserate,
but the animals rub their coats together.
They can move.
Can I?

The original void was stuffed
into our throats
we kept only
the first day and the
flowering spring was alien.

Deception

My love for you
Is nothing more than the dreary
Sound of the radio
No matter what I say
Your body too is disembodied
Your voice issues from nowhere
La nausée
Nothing can make me blush
Nothing can make me hope
My love for you started out as a stream
Of sparkling ice
melting under the reeling sun
It came as an untuned
song untaught and unaware
but now
after summer nights
some spent in uneasy bliss
and changing but similar days of night
subject to cold
and a rush of crowding seasons
released from the city's stone

now

it is nothing more than the hum of a sleazy song

on the radio

and as I listen inside my room

it draws from me the box of tears.

The Search

Who hopes

      in a vision

            alone.

Never

    have we experienced the

silver trance together

our eyes black

show

we are bent on the same search for

the river source

the same colours

within their nurtured vision

of the source its turquoise touch

I hope in

         the vision alone.

in my dream eye

I guess its cool

will touch and know I will know

when it flows

as lovers

couldn't we give

untouchable torrents touches of turquoise

to each other

bleeding   bleeding

the thick blue of love.

My Life in Two Worlds

In the other life I led
where the broken window leads inwards
crushed hope lay on my plate
above was the red sun at night
on your Parisian streets
sudden
hope ran wild eternity flowered
in every second I bled eternity
within you I became
the infinity of loss
no division between life and death.
Both cowered before my new vision.

Years later, in New York City, I saw
in your eyes you had never seen
what I had been given.
If we were in a story of my own
writing I would give you
my vision opening wilder than
infinite hope of rebirths, those gods
of any civilization within my human hand
driven images unwieldy within imagination
now such fresh blood under my touch.

I would give you what fear of
Death has taken from you.

Liaison

This wakening
  was not snug.
    It was a second when waiting broke
and flooded;
  eyes splintered
    and pricked the skin;
the body broke out of line
  and flickered with the speed
    of its own movement.
      My hunger declared itself
        so I had something to touch.
      While the heart beat too fast for purpose,
        shivering was no longer cold.

      It was then that I called out
      a low song
      and the ordinary miracle
      became part of the world.

All around was a hollow echo,
  my voice and my own voice.
I had something to touch,
  the wood, the pavement and flesh,
with horror came beauty
  and a moving home.

Touch Fall

I tried to touch myself
through you I fall.

I tried to touch
               to break
the sky   to see.
I tried into your body
               delve myself
to touch
     to be.

Out of my search a dead fish of remorse
eyes me hostilely
I dare not touch now
          you nor me.

The Gift

I was given a gift,
not flower, nor dress, not the perfect eye or mouth,
but a word, unheard.
Not a house or lover, nor the perfect sleep and waking,
but a mirror, unseen.

And when I searched
I could only see myself searching;
I could only see nothing,
Only the gift hiding its nothing in nothing.

Only in the streets did I find it,
when I did not search,
and the gift was in each flower,
dress, mouth, eye, sleeping and waking.

Only when I did not search,
did the gift, the unheard word, the mirror
shine.
Nothing shattered in the mind.

Imagining You

With my blood I made a silver lining
to every cloud that woke me each morning.
I made with my sinews a blessing
Of each evil encounter, loss and despairing
that came in disguise.
And eyeing the mirror I saw nothing
inside but the flat face
and no warmth but the cold gaze.

I was born
With my sinews, blood and eyesight and
sculpted a person
but lost him,
and in making him lost myself.
His body
wept on. His body torn up,
I wept, my body touching his severed limbs,
not for him but because there was nothing to hold
on to in storm.

Fidelity

because there was no one

                      else

only my child of your body

your body hard as a rose hip

you

    covered my eyes in your dreams

each morning I woke up

with words of colour

rainbowing through my open lids

it was

       beauty without construction

chance view of a flying lake

no bridge in sight

Incense

I kissed the night

             my reddened lips

             tasting the bitter cold

and blackened mist

I loosed my limbs

             their whiteness bare

             clear in the black night

Showing and yet unseen

But the incense of my body purged the sky

I drank the night

I ran in fear

             my spirit safe

             my spirit gone

I kissed the night.

The Return

I cannot return to

turn back to

fall slowly to earth

the soft clods do not coddle

the cradle bruises it

is too small

I break the wild flowering branches

And shred the pink blossom

sweet sickly sweet

are the picnics on the lawn.

The Body of Life

And then I know that the
only view is sheer darkness
and the deep descent downwards,
a narrow bridge breaking,
the wild sea on both sides.
With you, I already knew
that the exile from darkness,
the weaning from nothing,
was the only progression forwards.

On the branch of a winter tree,
on the shore of a milling city
By the window of an empty room,
I look from my blinkered eyes;
a white sky, a black sky,
it is not enough; it will not
content the searching.
The body of life is an old
woman, I must talk to
receive her heart.
She is silent; she is talking in
riddles; she is wandering.

She cannot remember her past.
I am trying to talk to her.
She will not hear me.
She has become the sea;
the bridge of words is breaking;
her black teeth are biting
the universe.
I am running, I have reached
the empty room,
The exile from darkness
The weaning from the woman of nothing
The knowledge of magnificent
emptiness.

I never tasted the fruit of the tree,
Only the common apple of
the land of sin,
and heard the babblings
of a dying woman.

In Your Soul

As the light falls down on me
As the light falls perfectly opening colour
hue of yellow pollen made liquid
the stitches of light die
holding this knowledge
infinity opens up as my hand's
touch
infinity opens up as a thought
without flesh
a pattern of waves
in a sea of my own making
and I say

I will go out
into this day
I will let hide despair
I will watch for the
light from another soul

My Lovers

He likes the moment before life stops;
the body before touching
falling from cliff to stone
the body almost white with below-living cold.
He likes those so delicate moments
before the bullet has reached flesh

                        and in his words

the dagger's brush
so delicately
precise.
On the other side is always woman
a woman
    who misses and betrays no outward sign
    of his skilled game,
    brushed by the wind of the knife's throw.

The Fall and Mourning of God

To be taken by God
who is of
     my own making
over the crest
     and mourning of his fall
bring me
     over the hump of this time
     these years
when singleness
is as life should touch
when the pain is the healing
and the old
     skin needs nothing
but to be left
which is the source of pain
to be left
which is the source of
       blood flowing
bring me
     beyond this too strong image
     which stops
me on the journey
till I can only look
back to what has passed

pull me or drag me
bring me and take me
      stand with me on the road
of moving
      which is the source of pain
  the shots continuing
in the back of the head
  return
alone

let me alone
to be taken by God
  who is of my own making
    over the crest and mourning of his fall.

Death

No more
air enters
motions your lips.

I cannot make clean the squalor.

But the many breaths
drawn from your life
come
to the rooms where you lived
fill them with quiet.

The many breaths
all your time past
passed to
        the drawers
littered
        each room
where I sit where you sat.

I cannot make clean the squalor.

There is
no more air.

Hope

Within
the transitory seed,
your warmth,
fires darkness, its blossoming.

The final achievement after time
is paradise.
The mystic knows
the infant's innocence
grows towards after-life
in sheath of hope.

And the man who lives in the act
  Loses face.
Underneath the vision is worn hollow
by the stones of time.

Icon of Giving

I

He took time from the sky
to hold me in his hands
which turn to cradle all.
See! I am learning the
movements of flesh and bone.
I am bent in cool thanks
but my hands are straight
spired with his breath;
my eyes are the starred
windows of his house,
jewels of light.

II

Before this icon of giving
I clenched my fists
Pointed one finger
used the nail to dig for nothing;
my movements shadowed
strange beasts on the nursery wall.

He took time from the sky
to hold me in his hands.

The Way

The way and the destination of heaven
Are airless,
Without substance.
There is no straight path
That flowers wild;
There is no city
To rest at on the way to the city
Celestial, not even in the limitless sky.
The way is curling,
Stony and seedy
Birds black flower in the
Coloured sky.

But the destination might
Be a flower whose smell
We awaken as we bend over her
Down in the early dawn.

Leave Me

You are probably right to leave me.
In Spring I am unleaving
I make the sky grey and my
Streams sound strained.
Clouds dream in their depths.
I have taken over the landscape in a horrible way
At a season of Spring Sprung.

Betrayal

Let these words
go beyond my room,
beyond the blackness,
stronger, because they have no more sound
being part of the air.
Let them touch your flesh,
though you are already lying in
thick embraces;
let the silent whistle ruffle
your dog hairs
and the scent will lead you.

Tonight darkness and winter
are exiled from my room;
they are moaning to get in;
let these words shrivel
in their spiteful grasp,
slip voiceless to your silent
tomb,
becoming, as no one comes,
frozen petals for a greying day.

Sense on My Skin

Put fire on clay to harden my memory;
Put sense on my skin;
Put love in me, but everyday,
or I will refuse it.
Never ask me to take flight in a
moment's bliss. Afterwards,
take me, but everyday, or
I will not love.

On Tête La Douleur Comme Une Bonne Louve

to let the summer be washed like a frescoe from the wall
to let the cold river of mud

        slide

          like a wedding-dress

over your limbs
wedded to rivers of night
to let

    to be forced to let
this leaving forever

       never regained

neither in warmth nor wine
to leave to cry
to hug

    this coldness close like a mother
to rock in the breast of unmerciful shudders
of cold
nor cradle calm

     to surrender one's hands up

     like a criminal

      saviour crossed

and be blotted neutral against the sky.

You Brought Invisible Flowers

You brought invisible flowers
 Like the ones I carry dried in my heart
  Only you see them with moist sense
   As we clasp the crying of tears
    Lights them up
     Dried blossoms flower spring rain
      If only you cried in my sight
       If only you broke down and cried.

Absence

The sadness empty sky
                    of another
Waking
          the infinite white
I feel senseless

river brown burning
black wastelands arise
wind glass-eyed
splinters unkind

The sadness of waking
                    you left and you left
the pain in spaces, hollows
the city, my mind
empty sky.

Rain to the Drought

The oblong door contains more
angles at right angles to each other,
hard and straight within
long lines.

My love who is unknown
To me blocks and curves
The straight lines
He changes; he is about
to walk out; he is
bursting with more
possibilities than
if I were to walk out without him.

My love is never here.
He is
the answer to the question,
the rain to the drought.
He about to walk out
and leave the straight lines
Static on the dull door.

This Still Line

This still line of my painting,
I know its tears.
There are pears and apples.
I have spent my brush
Polishing them so tranquil
For others.
There is nothing to eat on
my table.

This still line is of pain,
Do not remember it
I promised myself

But it returned.
I did not call it
I saw it
In pale colours
Though I refuse loneliness.

I will not cry as if believing
I am here to be hurt and alone.

A Dissident Replies

for those who stand
on the mountain of time
pretending to balance
with the earth up to their throats
    and look back and down
     containing in that second
    all years
     talking to the dead
    for those who collect the past

for those who ask questions
trying to link arm in arm
    all darkness to the blood
     trying to stick together
    the flesh that the pain pulls open
     trying to find a human word
    for the mystery

for all those who find life in the mind's
gyrating dance

I now join in making our excuses to the world.

Boundary Sight

My parents
traced out a path
of circles white chalk in the red
soil;
the first paths that carry the currents of wind,
the blue waves,
the circles of moon change swelling.

Too young I got caught in the whirlpool.
Out in the wide angular spaces I found the
endless plain like a blind
eternal shutter.
I lost the boundary sight,
the fire kept warm by circle.
Cowering,
I walked out.

Night entered my body which grew faint.
Miles of unchartered stone entered my mouth.
I spoke bleeding.
The circle,
ring on my finger, curve of my body,
got washed away, like a swimmer surfacing dead.

How I Am Stopped

With a hand of axe
I cut my life.
I stopped smelling the colours.
Only commands silencing all,
all I've done, over and over again.
It is living.
I have loved each day;
I have loved despite;
I can turn a circle in my imagination
on pointed toes while sitting still;
I can remember with precision
how you took your hand and hit my mother.

Separation

A ray of light

        shows through the ragged curtains,

        dusty as day,

        as the two figures,

                mother and child,

        that sit in silence,

in silence

        their years to come

        clutter empty cupboards and drawers.

The door is opened; the child walks out.

        gropes into particular details;

        daylight catches the colours

        of her face.

The door is opened. The mother walks out;

        child returns

        in the night; one figure

sits in silence, black as night.

Silent Prayer

The generation's song,
loosened by an old flow,
pulsed by the same sun,
is waiting
in the green stems plucking
its butterflies out
and is broken on the air
of cold shadow
or drips quietly on the dry roofs
and is not heard.
Only the bee and the waking tramp
reply silently.

The Waiting

There was always an air of waiting in the home.

What air we breathed was not enough;

Only the powerful pulse of our

Dreams, not god,

Gave us some hope. What we

had was as meagre

As our dreams were large.

Now we come out into the light of day

Which is neither what was

nor what we hoped would be.

The colours are different

And even death has a new form.

Inside My Love

Inside my love there is someone
who finds it strange to be called a human being,
to be told he is near the creator,
a mongrel born of heaven and soil
coming and returning to each in turn;
a mongrel with the chance
of his half-blood blossoming in rebirth.

Inside my love there is I
who watch his being, glancing
anxiously at the full-bred stone
and perhaps the dog who is not
tottering between soil and earth sky,
the stone that is
and does not see
the minutes of losing
the erosion of all feeling, all except
the end of feeling,
the stone that is being
while he remains blind with his sight.

Inside my love is she
who is rooted not to the soil
in the plant's immobility
but to the moving giddiness of half knowing,
rooted also to a hundred beckonings
that paralyse
take one to another patch of soil.

Inside my love is a man who
lies under the movement of his own body
who lies under another's body
to find ecstasy in the undivided
being of the stone
who does not know that I am watching him

Our Touch

slowly
the day drips into my hand its juice
leaving the fruit more full

slowly
the day softens in moist haze
bright stiff colour
lose and loosen
                    on my eye
slowly I wipe off the dust
with each tear
                    squeezed
from the core by warmth
of seeing with you

slowly
so slowly the tears touch
to light
            our touch.

Save Me

I half

    become

        you (as you)

          tell me

    half unknown

I search in you

For stranger

Selves

Myself

But the night will swallow me

If I let lightness in

But the night will enter me

If I let lightness in

And heaviness will

Fall on my by night.

Can you see

eyes   eyes?

As the cliff mocks my fall

Through air

No mind

With its beetle writing legs as it struggles to rise

Can come between me and the earth

Can save me.

Mother

mother, you left,
you left
my bedroom, my window, my
body open onto
the black blow of the spawn-specked night.
mother,
I have lain night long
feeling the rough claw-marks
of winter time
on my flesh.

I have lain -
out of the window
the dead-white landscape
rustles its withered
trees
their lucid shadows
electric white
cover with substanceless sheets
my body.

night-long
the landscape of severed hopes -
grey corn, clay sheaths
perfumeless broken shell -
rough-edged
entered through
the open window, my eyes.

mother, you left.
Thank you for leaving the
window open for my escape.
Come and see as I make
my lurching leap out
to the black night
shelled earth.

mother you left me.
I leave myself now.

Continuing Past

I

In the night of black violence,
I was sculptured in your arms.
The covers thrown off to the once
mirroring all-night black
was animal fur to flesh,
and each had separate smell.

II

The first painting was
madonna and child and man's God
spoke in his Image.
He died, but this remains.

III

The first tears dripped
to shadows shrouded by metal bars
pulsing to centre of chain,
passing inwards and out
to a sluggish current of past time.
The falcon on his master's wrist was more free,
than the shadows that sucked death's milk
from the first tear pools.
They milked Prometheus' rock of tears
less free than the falcon.

IV

In the night of our violence
a lady was sitting close by.
The rust of the chain reddened her hair
and smells arose older than the ancient shadow and root
Her shadows creepered the walls
Her people were walking the walls.

V

Where is the Season?
For the same image of Spring
can return without the season's call
Where is the painting?
For the first painting has already
gathered the shadows to last.
Where is the only true voice?
It is only a note in continuing past
of more than echo.
The falcon would not falcon
if freed from the master's wrist.
Would she fly to the wind's call
Or flounder in a river's song?

VI

The season is blossoming.

The image of mother and child,

are far from the first cradle wandering.

As the night of black violence sculptures in silence,

the day is dawning on earth reversed.

The Rationale

I cannot let life
lie on my soul
the lover's words
lie with my soul.

The weight crushes
small mind
pinned and pulled apart
by each second's change.

Each second
new leaving
bleached and discoloured
joy.

I cannot let life
fall on my soul.

Brush Strokes Of Sex

so is this thick
unnatural blue
stretching a horizontal
zone
between nothing and nothing
a bridge without
base
so thick
its substance of waiting dream
that cannot take seed on this earth
yet weighing
this earth, this sky
with a dull moan
to be let out
filling the self-made vacuum
life
with an added blindness
till it serves the day
with its own beauty -
distance -
want.

unlike
the vertical
sudden the flight through air

that for one moment

nothing is felt

only this speed of falling

as your hand, forbidden,

enters my leg.

There is laughter.

The blood shed is not real.

Hear As...

Hear as
the flower blossoms
silence of awe
there is no imagining more
beautiful and no words
describe this
woman

for Joe with love

All

You held me like a man
and a woman
a mother paddling her child
on the shore of a sea that
would become eyes of the waves

you led me without words

you pulled my body over
oceans my mind wept wept
tears under my arms and thighs
so many weepings for all I
had never lost

you walked me to the
crossroads where all
blood flows

and all round I had eyes
everywhere

Touching Earth

Will my voice break further
in the throat, the expression
made less adolescent,
for there are castle walls
thick brick that will not hear me.
Each time I come here, new rulers
shuffle, in inaccessible games
complacent, once hunters now the republic.
And still, I come to them
wanting to sit beloved in the
cold stone of their possessed place.
I return to the same dream
for it was never a place with a door.
And as I talk there half
in tears, half unconcerned,
wandering elsewhere in my mind
I see the palette of some sky
smashed in irreconcilable
colours to splash harmony
relentless in pink violet
of light.

The colours were never placed
but streamed in power; I watched
dropping my questions like pebbles
aimlessly to hear the sound
they make touching earth.

Mirage

My ancestors are shadow,
so embrace this with mine.
My enemies are shadow;
I have learnt their language
which is stronger than silence.

The only embrace to grow vision
takes time to learn
and perhaps music to move
the body's rhythm.

Slowly take this climate that
is too sunless to win flowers
and fire it to colour.
They are painters on my empty canvas
who eat my flesh.

Let us sit in a café caring
for nothing but this mirage.

Being Of Two

The two worlds
come together
Tensing to touch the
Second of coming to being

This being of two
Plunders the sky and
The earth of all passion
And colour and force

The two worlds
Unite present with past
Till the scars of severed
Childhood and birth
Are soothed, softened away

In the rush of the first
River rain
And the old landscape appears out of blue mist.

Contents

List of Plates

Paintings by Melinda Camber Porter